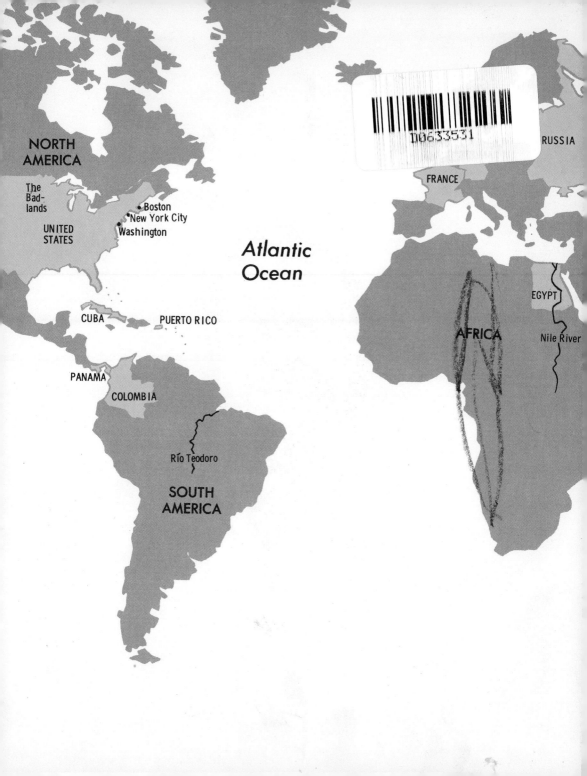

NORTH
AMERICA

The
Bad-
lands

UNITED
STATES

• Boston
• New York City
Washington

Atlantic
Ocean

CUBA   PUERTO RICO

PANAMA

COLOMBIA

Río Teodoro

SOUTH
AMERICA

RUSSIA

FRANCE

EGYPT

AFRICA   Nile River

MEET
Theodore Roosevelt

By ORMONDE DE KAY, JR.

Illustrated by JACK DAVIS

Step-Up Books ⌐_⌐ Random House
New York

For Lenore and Philip

Contents

1 Meet Theodore Roosevelt   **3**

2 His Father, Lincoln, and the North   **7**

3 School Books and Notebooks   **11**

4 A Museum Starts With a Seal   **15**

5 Teedie Grows Up   **19**

6 Theodore At College   **22**

7 Into Politics   **27**

8 The Young Assemblyman   **30**

9 The Terrible Day   **35**

10 The Wild West   **39**

11 Bad News From the Badlands   **42**

12 "Remember the Maine!"   **46**

13 Rough Rider Roosevelt   **50**

14 "The Big Stick"   **55**

15 The Youngest President   **59**

16 The Square Deal   **67**

17 The Panama Canal   **70**

18 T.R. Keeps the Peace   **75**

19 Strong As a Bull Moose   **79**

20 The Old Lion   **82**

21 After Theodore Roosevelt   **86**

1
MEET
THEODORE ROOSEVELT

Theodore Roosevelt was President of the United States from 1901 to 1909. He was one of the liveliest men who ever lived. Whenever he laughed, everyone else laughed, too.

In his busy life, Roosevelt was a soldier, writer, explorer, and lion hunter. He was even a cowboy!

Roosevelt loved life. And he loved America. Americans remember him as a great President who worked hard to make his country stronger and better.

Theodore Roosevelt was born in New York City, New York, in 1858. In 1858 there were 32 states in the United States. New York State had more people than any other state. And New York City had more people than any other American city.

America was growing fast. People kept coming from Europe to New York. Some stayed to work in the city's factories and stores. Others joined the Americans going west. They went to Middle Western states to farm, or to California to look for gold. Or they went to places that were not yet states. There they might help build railways, or dig for gold and silver, or raise cattle.

In 1858 few people were going to the southern states. There was not much land or work for them in the South. Negro slaves worked the big cotton farms called plantations. The slave owners gave the slaves food and clothes, but little or no money.

Theodore Roosevelt's mother was named Martha. She came from the South. His father came from New York City in the North. There they lived in a tall brownstone house.

In 1855 Martha had a baby girl, Anna, who was nicknamed Bamie. On October 27, 1858, Martha had a baby boy. Mr. Roosevelt gave the boy his own name, Theodore. The new baby's nickname was Teedie.

2

HIS FATHER, LINCOLN, AND THE NORTH

Teedie was not a healthy boy. He had a sickness called asthma. His asthma often made it hard for him to breathe. His father would take Teedie in his arms and walk up and down the room until the boy could breathe more easily.

As Teedie grew up he became very close to his father. Mr. Roosevelt sometimes talked to him about a war being fought in the United States. It was called the Civil War.

The President of the United States was Abraham Lincoln. He was from the North. The southern planters were afraid he might try to put an end to slavery. So they set up their own government. Lincoln had said all the states must stay under one government. And a war had begun between the southern states and the northern states. It was a long and terrible war.

Mrs. Roosevelt wanted the South to win. But Mr. Roosevelt wanted the North to win. Teedie was for his father, Lincoln, and the North.

One night he prayed aloud to God to grind the soldiers of the South to powder.

On April 9, 1865, the North won the war. All the slaves would soon be freed. All the states were under one government again. Lincoln was Teedie's hero.

But five days later, a southerner killed Lincoln in Washington, the capital of the country. Lincoln's body was put in a coffin and taken in a train through the North. In New York City horses pulled the coffin slowly through the streets.

Teedie saw it go by. He saw people standing with their heads bowed. Some of them were crying. Teedie thought Lincoln must have been a great man for people to care about him so much.

3
SCHOOL BOOKS AND NOTEBOOKS

By this time Teedie had a little brother, Elliott, and a little sister, Conie. He played with them in the yard behind the Roosevelts' house. But his asthma kept bothering him. He was sick too often to go to a school, as his big sister Bamie did.

But Mrs. Roosevelt's sister Annie was living with the family. She was a good teacher. She taught Teedie, Elliott, and Conie to read and write and do sums. The children's first school was at home.

The Roosevelt children were lucky to have any school at all. In those days many children had to work from early morning till dark. Their fathers and mothers needed the money they earned to buy food. But Mr. Roosevelt was rich. Every summer he took his family away to the country.

Teedie had fun in the country. He ran barefoot across the fields. He made a wigwam in the woods. He swam in ponds and lakes.

The Roosevelt children had dogs and cats. They had a raccoon and a pony. Teedie loved to play with the pets. He also liked to watch wild animals, birds, and insects.

One day he lay on the ground to watch some ants. Then he took his notebook and wrote about them. He said there were three kinds of ants. He said some ants were officers, some soldiers, and some workers.

He did not spell well. He wrote "soilder" for "soldier". But what he wrote showed that he was thinking about what he saw.

4
A MUSEUM STARTS
WITH A SEAL

One day in New York City, Teedie was passing a fish store when he saw a dead seal on a box. He knew seals were not good to eat. So this one could only be there for show.

Suddenly Teedie wanted the seal more than anything. He asked the fish man if he could have it. The fish man just laughed. But Teedie kept coming back to ask for the seal.

15

Soon the seal began to smell bad. The fish man knew he would have to get rid of it. He told Teedie to come back the next day. Teedie did. The fish man gave him the seal's head bone, or skull.

Teedie was very happy. He had an idea. He would get together lots of living and dead animals. He would start his own zoo and museum.

He began to hunt. In the city he hunted in parks. In the country he hunted everywhere. He caught mice, frogs, and turtles. He caught many small animals. Some he kept alive in his room. Others he killed and skinned. And he put the skins away with his seal skull.

When he was ten, the family went in a ship to Europe. Teedie had to leave his collection behind. The Roosevelts visited beautiful old cities in many lands. But Teedie did not have much fun. His asthma was bad. And he missed the United States.

One day his mother showed him a letter from New York. With it was a photograph of a girl he knew named Edith Carow. Her photograph made him feel more homesick than ever.

At last the family sailed home. Teedie wrote in his notebook how glad he was to get back to his own country. "This morning we saw land of America and went in to the bay. New York!!! Hip! Hurrah!"

5
TEEDIE GROWS UP

Because Teedie could not run and play much, he was thin and weak. His father worried about him. One day Mr. Roosevelt had a talk with his son. He told him he needed a stronger body. Then he took him to the second floor of the house.

There, a big room in the back had been turned into a gym. It had a punching bag and a swing. It had two bars on which Teedie could lift himself to make his arms strong.

Soon Teedie was going to the gym every day. He chinned himself. He did push-ups. He lifted weights. It was hard, boring work. But, little by little, he grew stronger.

In the country, Teedie liked to go hunting with friends. He was 13 now, and he had a rifle. But one day he found he could not read a sign which the others could read. His eyesight was bad. So he began to wear glasses. Now he could see well. He became a good shot.

When he killed something he no longer just skinned it. He made a framework of wire and clay and put it inside the skin. The animal or bird looked almost alive after that.

Soon Teedie had a chance to add strange new birds to his collection. The whole family took a trip to the land of Egypt. There they hired a houseboat. They sailed up the Nile River. Teedie was having much too much fun to feel homesick. Even his asthma did not spoil his fun.

After Egypt, the family went to Europe again for a long stay. When Teedie got home, he was 15. He felt too grown up for his baby name. He wanted to be called Theodore.

6

THEODORE AT COLLEGE

When Theodore was 17 he went to Harvard College, near Boston. The other boys at Harvard thought he was strange. He kept snakes and turtles in his room. He was always excited about something. Instead of walking, he seemed to bounce. The Harvard boys said he would never be a quiet young gentleman, like them.

But Theodore did not care much what they said. He was too busy. He read many books and played many games. He liked boxing best of all. He loved a good, clean fight.

In time the other boys got used to him. They came to like him.

During Theodore's second year at Harvard, his father died. Theodore thought his father was the best man he had ever known. It was a sad blow. But his father had taught him never to give in to sadness. So he set to work writing a book.

His book was about a war between the United States and England, the War of 1812. In that war many battles had been fought on the sea.

Theodore had to learn a lot about the Navy and its warships to write the book.

On vacations he often hunted with his brother, Elliott. They went after bigger game now. They hunted deer and bears. And they hunted one of the biggest American animals of all, the moose.

One day at Harvard a friend took Theodore to a party. There he met a girl who lived near Boston. Her name was Alice Lee. He thought she was the prettiest girl he had ever seen. Theodore fell in love with her. He asked her to marry him.

For a year she would not say yes or no. Theodore was very unhappy. But he kept on asking her. At last she said yes.

Theodore finished his four years at Harvard in June of 1880. And on October 27 he married Alice Lee. It was his 22nd birthday.

7
INTO POLITICS

Theodore and Alice went to live with his mother in New York City. It was a wonderful winter. They went to many parties. They skated. And they took long sleigh rides in the park.

Theodore was rich. He did not have to work. But he wanted to be useful. So he began to study law.

The men who make laws are in government. Theodore knew their work was very important. He wanted to get into government work himself.

The best way for him to start was to join a political party. There are two big political parties in America, the Republicans and the Democrats. Theodore's two heroes, his father and Lincoln, had been Republicans. So he joined a Republican Club.

The men at the Club were not at all like his Harvard friends. They were a much tougher crowd. But Theodore liked them. They worked hard to get the people to vote for Republicans.

In New York City, most people voted for Democrats. In other parts of New York State, Republicans won most elections.

Theodore knew one reason why Democrats won city elections. They took money from the city. And they paid people to vote for them.

Theodore knew it was not right to take money from the government, or buy votes. But as a Republican, he could not do much to make the city government any better.

One day a Republican leader came to Theodore. He asked him to run for the State Assembly. If he were elected, he could help make state laws. Theodore said he would run.

8
THE YOUNG ASSEMBLYMAN

Theodore went into the streets to talk to the people. He asked them to vote for him. He said he would get them better laws if they would elect him to the Assembly.

Politicians always say things like that. But the people could tell that Theodore meant what he said.

He did not look like a politician.
His clothes were too fancy. And he
did not sound like a politician. His
voice was high, and he had a funny
way of talking. But on Election Day
he got twice as many votes as the
Democrat who ran against him. He
was elected!

So Theodore became Mr. Theodore Roosevelt, Assemblyman. He went with Alice in a train to Albany, the capital of New York State. There he found that the state government was not much better than the city government. And some of the worst men in it were Republicans.

These men did little for the people who had elected them. Instead, they worked for rich men who owned big businesses. The big businessmen gave them money. Then they made laws to help the big businessmen.

Roosevelt thought this was as bad as buying votes. He wanted to do something about it. At last he got his chance.

He heard that a big businessman had paid a state judge to help him take over a railway. If this was so, the judge was breaking a state law. Roosevelt asked the assemblymen to find out the truth.

The assemblymen said the judge had done no wrong. But plenty of people thought Roosevelt had been right. He was elected again, twice.

In the fall of 1883, Alice told him she was going to have a baby. She went to stay with his mother. On February 13, 1884, Elliott sent him news in Albany. Alice had had a baby girl. Roosevelt ran to catch a train to New York City.

9
THE TERRIBLE DAY

In the city Roosevelt went right to his mother's house. Elliott came to the door. His eyes were red. He had been crying.

"There is a curse on this house," he said. "Mother is dying, and Alice is dying, too."

Roosevelt looked at his brother in horror. Then he rushed upstairs.

What Elliott had said was true. At about three o'clock in the morning of February 14, Martha Roosevelt died. And at about two o'clock that afternoon, Alice Roosevelt died.

In one day Roosevelt had lost his mother and his wife. It was almost too terrible a blow for him to bear. But he pulled himself together. He went back to Albany. And he kept on working for better government.

In his work, he found out a lot about big businessmen. They owned all kinds of businesses the country needed. Roosevelt knew they were helping to build up the country. But he felt they had no right to so much political power.

So he wrote new laws to make big businessmen less powerful. After a hard fight, he got the assemblymen to pass them. The governor, Grover Cleveland, was a Democrat. But he signed the laws. So they became laws of New York State.

It was a big victory for Roosevelt. But he was still sad about losing his wife and his mother. When the Assembly finished its work for the year, he left New York State. He went west.

He went to the Dakota Territory, now the states of North and South Dakota. There, in a beautiful and wild place called the Badlands, he bought a ranch.

10
THE WILD WEST

The cowboys on Roosevelt's ranch did not know what to think of their boss. He never smoked. He never drank whiskey. And his only swear words were "By George!" The cowboys decided he was just a sissy from the East.

One night Roosevelt met a wild cowboy with a gun in each hand. The cowboy teased him about his glasses. He called him "Four Eyes." Roosevelt grinned. Then he hit the cowboy hard. Both guns went off in the air. And the cowboy fell to the floor, out cold.

Roosevelt and his men were soon good friends. He rode on horseback with them to round up the cattle. And as he breathed the dry western air, his asthma left him forever.

Roosevelt loved the West. He went hunting all over the wild western country. But he saw things that worried him. He saw wide fields of stumps, where trees had been cut down for railway ties or firewood. If this kept up, the woods would be gone. The animals and birds would be gone, too. The beautiful West would become an ugly wasteland.

Roosevelt felt this must never be allowed to happen. But he was not sure just how it could be stopped.

Sometimes Roosevelt went East to see his little girl, Alice, and his sisters, Bamie and Conie. Visiting Bamie in New York City, he met Edith Carow again. She was the girl whose picture had made him homesick as a boy. He and Edith fell in love.

Then Roosevelt had a bad defeat. He ran for mayor of New York City against two men. The Democrat won. But Roosevelt did not even come in second. He came in last of all.

Edith had gone across the sea to England. Roosevelt went after her. He married her. And he brought her to his new home near New York City. It was called Sagamore Hill.

11
BAD NEWS FROM
THE BADLANDS

That winter bad news came from
the Badlands. Great storms had
covered the ground with snow.
Cold winds had turned the snow to
ice. The cattle had had no grass or
hay to eat. Most of them were dead.

Roosevelt had to sell his ranch. His days as a cattleman were over. And he had lost so badly in his try for mayor of New York that his days as a politician seemed over. But his book about the War of 1812 was well liked. So he began to write again.

He started work on his greatest book, "The Winning of the West." It told of how Americans had gone west, fought Indians, and settled the land.

While Roosevelt wrote, the West was still being won. More and more people were going to new western states like North and South Dakota.

Many things were happening at Sagamore Hill, too.

In September of 1887, Edith had a baby boy. Roosevelt did just what his father had done. He named the boy Theodore, after himself.

Next year he was back in politics. President Benjamin Harrison made him a civil service commissioner in the United States government.

The civil service is made up of the people who carry on the daily work of the government. Politicians often gave jobs to people just because they were their friends. Roosevelt thought this was wrong. He made people who wanted jobs in the government take a test to show they could do the work. The civil service became better.

As a civil service commissioner, Roosevelt lived in Washington. His family grew bigger there. Edith had a second boy, Kermit. She had a girl, Ethel. And she had a third boy, Archie.

In 1893 Grover Cleveland became President. He was a Democrat. But he liked Roosevelt's work in the civil service. He asked Roosevelt to stay on.

Roosevelt stayed two more years. Then the mayor of New York City asked him to be commissioner of police. The job sounded exciting. So Roosevelt gave up his job in the civil service. He left Washington. And he went to New York City.

12
"REMEMBER THE MAINE!"

New York's police had never had such an active boss. After a long day's work Roosevelt might take Edith out to a party. After dinner he would leave. He would dash all over the city, making sure the policemen were doing their work.

Often, a newspaper writer named Jacob Riis went along. Riis showed Roosevelt parts of the city he had never seen. In the slums Roosevelt saw houses full of rats. He saw a room where two big families had to sleep, eat, and do their work.

He wanted to help the poor people. So did Riis. Riis wrote about the slums. The people read his stories in their newspapers. They became upset, too. They urged the mayor to clean up the slums.

Roosevelt used newspapers to tell the people many of his ideas. He became well known. When he went back to Washington in 1897, the New Yorkers were sorry to see him go.

The country had a new President named William McKinley. He was a Republican. He made Roosevelt his assistant secretary of the Navy. Roosevelt's new job had to do with Navy warships and the islands they visited in two oceans.

The Philippine Islands, in the Pacific Ocean, belonged to Spain. Near America in the Atlantic Ocean, Spain had two more islands. They were Puerto Rico and Cuba.

In Cuba, the Spanish were very cruel to the people. For years the Cubans had been fighting them to be free. Most Americans wanted the Cubans to win. So did Roosevelt. He was all for them.

In February of 1898 the American warship Maine was visiting Cuba. One night it blew up. Many sailors died. No one knows why the Maine blew up. But Roosevelt and many other people blamed the Spanish.

Some newspapers called for a war. "Remember the Maine! Down with Spain!" people shouted. In April, America went to war with Spain.

Roosevelt became a lieutenant colonel in the Army. He called for men to join his regiment. From all over the country they came. There were cowboys, college boys, Indians, and hundreds of others. Roosevelt and his men were called the Rough Riders. By June they were in Cuba.

13
ROUGH RIDER ROOSEVELT

On July 2, Colonel Roosevelt and his Rough Riders lay in high grass. They were hiding from the Spanish soldiers on top of a nearby hill. An American soldier handed Roosevelt a note from the general. Roosevelt was to capture the hill.

He jumped onto his horse. "Come on, boys!" he shouted. He rode up the hill. His men ran after him.

Spanish bullets whizzed through the air. Many Americans were hit. Many fell. But the rest kept going. When they were near the top of the hill, the Spanish soldiers ran away. The Rough Riders cheered their brave "Colonel Teddy."

Soon Spain gave up. Cuba became a free country. America took over Puerto Rico and the Philippines. And the Hawaiian Islands in the Pacific became American at their own wish. Roosevelt was delighted.

But the ending of the war did not mean all was well. In Cuba there was a deadly sickness called yellow fever. Roosevelt watched his men fall sick and die, one after another.

He felt sad about the men. And he was angry at the Army. He wrote to his general. He said the men must leave Cuba right away. Newspapers printed his letter. The American people grew angry too. They wanted the army to send the soldiers home.

At last, ships came. Roosevelt and his Rough Riders sailed north to a camp near New York City. There he said good-by to his men. Some men cried as they said good-by.

When Roosevelt got home, he was surprised to find that everyone had read about his fighting in Cuba. He was a hero.

One day a man named Thomas Platt came to see him. Platt ran the Republican party in New York State. He asked Roosevelt to run for governor. Roosevelt went all over the state. He gave talks in big cities and small towns. The people listened. In November, 1898, they elected him to be their governor.

14
"THE BIG STICK"

Soon Platt began to wish someone else were governor. He was used to telling Republican governors what to do. But Governor Roosevelt ran the state his own way.

He knew that some lawmakers took money from big businessmen. They made laws to help businesses. Platt did not think this was wrong at all. But Roosevelt did. He thought laws should help everyone, not just a few rich men.

So the Republican governor and the Republican boss argued.

As governor, Roosevelt had great power. He could take state jobs away from Platt's friends. He could even turn down new laws he did not like. His power made him think of a wise saying from Africa. The saying was "Speak softly and carry a big stick."

Governor Roosevelt's "big stick" was his power. He did not have to shout at Platt to get his way. His "big stick" let him win most of the arguments.

By "speaking softly and carrying a big stick," he got the lawmakers to make good laws. One law made big businessmen pay tax money to the state. Another made them pay money to workers hurt on the job.

News of Roosevelt's work spread. Americans already knew of him as a war hero. Now they talked of him as a politician who got things done.

In 1900 McKinley was sure to run for President again. But who would run with him for Vice President? Many Republicans wanted Roosevelt. Platt was one. If Roosevelt was in Washington, Platt could run the Republicans in New York again.

In July Republicans from all the states met. They picked Roosevelt for Vice President. Platt was glad.

In November the Republicans won the election. Roosevelt, it seemed, would be the Vice President for the next four years.

15

THE YOUNGEST PRESIDENT

Roosevelt's new job bored him. A Vice President does not have much power. But America needs a Vice President. If the President dies, the Vice President takes his place.

In the spring of 1901, Roosevelt left Washington for a long vacation at Sagamore Hill. There he wrote parts of "The Winning of the West" over again. And he spent a lot of time with his children. He played football with them. He went riding on horseback with them. And he told them wonderful stories.

Roosevelt had six children by now. Alice was 17, Theodore Junior, 14. Kermit was 12, Ethel was 10, and Archie was 7. Last came Quentin, 3. Theodore Roosevelt, storyteller and Vice President, was 42 years old.

The Roosevelts loved to do things together. In late summer of 1901 they visited the mountains of New York State. President McKinley was also in the state, in Buffalo. On September 6, he was shot by a man who hated all governments.

Roosevelt hurried to Buffalo. The President lay in bed. His doctors were afraid he might die. But five days after the shooting, they said he would be all right.

Roosevelt went back to his family.

On September 13, he and his two older boys climbed a mountain. On their way down they heard shots. Was it a signal? Roosevelt fired a gun to show where he was. Soon, a man came running up with news.

The President was much worse.

Late that night another man rode up to the house where the family was staying. He brought a short note. "The President is dying," it said. "Come at once."

Roosevelt jumped to the seat of a waiting wagon. The driver cracked his whip and the horses started off. They raced over bumpy roads, hour after hour.

It was almost daylight when they stopped at a little railway station. A train with only one car stood on the tracks. A man hurried over to Roosevelt. "The President is dead," he said. Roosevelt climbed into the car and the little train moved off.

The train pulled into Buffalo that afternoon. Roosevelt went first to the house where McKinley's body lay. There he said his last good-by.

Then he went to meet the men who had been closest to McKinley in the government.

The men shook his hand. Then a judge came up to him with a Bible. Roosevelt put his left hand on the Bible and held up his right hand. He swore to uphold the country's laws. And so, Theodore Roosevelt became the 26th President of the United States.

When Platt heard the news, he was upset. Now President Roosevelt was the most powerful man in the whole country. He carried a bigger "big stick" than anyone else.

Big businessmen were afraid the new President might use his "big stick" on them. He might stop them from buying the votes of lawmakers in the United States government. He might stop them from making money in ways that were against the laws of the country.

But most Americans were not at all upset. They thought that good times were coming. For they liked Roosevelt, the youngest President America had ever had.

16
THE SQUARE DEAL

The White House, quiet old home of Presidents, was now loud with the shouts of Roosevelt's children. At bedtime President Roosevelt had wild pillow fights with his children. Famous men had to wait to see him.

At dinner senators and other top men in the government met cowboys, Rough Riders, newspapermen and teachers. One great teacher who came to dinner was named Booker T. Washington. He was a Negro. Until the Civil War, he had been a slave.

Some people were angry that the President had dined with a Negro. He said they were silly. Later, he said in a talk that all Americans should have a "Square Deal." And he showed what he meant.

Often men who owned businesses of the same kind got together. They made one huge business, or trust. One trust owned all the railways in the Northwest. This trust charged people a lot of money for using the railways. And the people had to pay. They had no choice.

Roosevelt used laws to break the power of the Northwestern railway trust. Its owners had to lower the fare. The people had a Square Deal.

Later, the men who dug coal said they needed more money. The mine owners would not even talk about it. So the miners stopped work.

Roosevelt knew that many people would die of cold without coal for their fires. He grew angry. He got newspapermen to tell just how pig-headed the mine owners were being. The people grew angry, too.

At last the mine owners agreed to talk. The miners won more pay and went back to work. Both the miners and the people had a Square Deal.

Powerful men fought the Square Deal. But Roosevelt remembered to "Speak softly and carry a big stick." Most of the time he had his way.

17
THE PANAMA CANAL

Roosevelt's "big stick" for dealing
with other countries was the Navy.
He made the Navy bigger and better.
He loved to go to sea and watch the
big white Navy ships go by.

America needed warships to guard its new islands. In the Philippines, Filipinos were fighting Americans. The American governor, William Howard Taft, was trying to bring peace to the islands. And the Navy was sending him help.

But to get to the Philippines from the Atlantic Ocean, ships had to go all the way around South America. Could a shorter way be found?

Roosevelt thought so. He wanted a waterway or canal dug between the Atlantic and Pacific Oceans. Ships could go straight through it.

The best place to dig was Panama, where North and South America join. Panama is only a few miles wide. In 1904 Panama belonged to Colombia, in South America.

A French company had started a Panama canal, then given up. But it still owned the rights to dig the canal. Roosevelt bought the rights with government money. He said Colombia could have some money, too. But Colombia wanted more. So Roosevelt had to think of another way to get the land for the canal.

Secretly, he met with a man from the French canal company. The man went to Panama. He stirred up the Panamanians to fight Colombia. The government of Colombia sent an army to Panama in ships.

But Roosevelt had already sent warships to Panama. They kept the Colombian ships away. Colombian soldiers could not land. So Panama won. Its government said America could start digging the canal.

Many Americans did not like this. They said Roosevelt had used his "big stick" too hard on Colombia. But in 1904 the people elected him President again, with more votes than any man before him.

18

T.R. KEEPS THE PEACE

Americans liked Roosevelt so well they called him T.R., or Teddy. The toy Teddy bear was named after him. With his wide grin, he seemed a bit like a big, friendly bear himself.

But some people thought he liked war too much. He surprised them. He showed he was a man of peace.

In 1905 Russia and Japan were at war with each other. T.R. asked both countries to send men to the United States. Some Russians and some Japanese came. T.R. brought them together for talks. At last, they agreed to end the war.

People all over the world said T.R. had done a great thing. By making peace, he had saved many lives.

The fighting in the Philippines was over now, too. T.R. called Taft back to Washington. He made Taft secretary of war. T.R.'s plan for keeping the country out of war was simple. It was to keep the country always ready for war. Then other countries would not dare to attack the United States or its islands.

In 1907 T.R. put his plan to work. He sent 16 big warships all the way around the world. They were called the Great White Fleet. They showed off American power on the sea. And America stayed at peace.

All this time T.R. kept on giving Americans a Square Deal. He broke up trusts that became too powerful. This was called "trust-busting."

In the West, railway and other trusts were cutting down beautiful forests. T.R. could not stand this waste. To stop it, he turned forests into National Parks. In the parks, no one can cut down trees or hunt. Birds and animals live in peace. Millions of people visit the great National Parks. They belong to all Americans, forever.

In 1908 most Republicans wanted T.R. for President again. But T.R. got them to pick Taft. Taft became President. And T.R. went hunting.

19
STRONG AS A BULL MOOSE

T.R. went to Africa with his son Kermit. They killed lions and other wild animals. And they sent the skins to a museum in Washington.

Once, T.R. shot a rhinoceros. It was hurt, but it charged straight at him. T.R. shot it again. It still kept coming. T.R. held his breath. When the huge animal was just a few feet from him, it fell dead.

After almost a year of hunting, the two men went to Egypt. There, Mrs. Roosevelt and Ethel joined them. The four Roosevelts sailed happily together down the Nile River.

From Egypt they went to Europe. In every city people cheered them. Kings and queens asked them to stay in their castles. Europeans all wanted to meet the great American, Theodore Roosevelt.

And when the Roosevelts' ship came to New York City, Americans shouted for joy. T.R. was surely the best-loved man in all America.

Home at Sagamore Hill, T.R. saw old friends and read newspapers. He did not like what he heard and read about President Taft. He knew Taft was a good, hard-working man. But he felt Taft listened to the big businessmen too much instead of getting on with "trust-busting."

Big businessmen and their friends in the Republican party liked Taft. In 1912 they picked him to run for President again. But many other Republicans wanted T.R. to run. So they started a new party called the Progressive party. They asked T.R. if he would run for President as a Progressive. He said he would. He was very excited.

The Progressives had another name. Once a man asked T.R. how he felt. T.R. said he felt as strong as a bull moose. The Progressives were nicknamed the Bull Moosers.

The Democrats picked Woodrow Wilson to run for President.

20
THE OLD LION

On October 14, 1912, T.R. was in
Milwaukee, Wisconsin, to give a talk.
As he got into a car, a man shot
him in the chest. T.R. fell back.
Men grabbed the gunman. But T.R.
shouted, "Stop! Don't hurt him!"

Policemen took the gunman away. Someone put a bandage over T.R.'s chest. T.R. went to the hall where he was to speak. He pulled out the pages of his talk. The bullet had drilled a hole through them. The thick papers had slowed the bullet. They had saved T.R.'s life.

T.R.'s wound left him weak. But he would not give up running for President. He went all over America. He told people about his plans for making the government better.

In the election T.R. beat Taft by almost a million votes. But Wilson, the Democrat, got even more votes than T.R. So Wilson was elected President.

A year later, T.R. went to South America. He led some men down a river through wild jungles. His men made the first map of the river. So the river was named Río Teodoro, the River of Theodore.

In 1914 war broke out in Europe. France and England fought Germany. And in 1917 America joined the war on the side of France and England.

T.R. asked President Wilson to let him fight in France. But T.R. could not hear well. He was blind in one eye from a boxing accident. He was often sick. So Wilson said no.

T.R. felt useless, like an old lion too sick to hunt. But he was proud that his sons could fight for their country. Theodore Junior was hurt. So was Archie. Quentin was killed. That news almost killed T.R., too.

On November 11, 1918, Germany gave up. The war was over. Archie was sent home to get well. But T.R. was sicker than anyone knew. Early on January 6, 1919, he died.

Archie sent his brothers in France five words: "The old lion is dead."

21
AFTER THEODORE ROOSEVELT

Today, Cuba and the Philippines both have their own governments. Puerto Rico is still American, but it runs itself. And the Hawaiian Islands are the State of Hawaii.

But people do not usually think of islands when they think of T.R. They think of his big grin and his bouncy ways. They think of him "trust-busting" with a "big stick."

Roosevelt hoped to be remembered for the Panama Canal. He is. But many people remember him better for the National Parks. They call the parks his finest memorial.

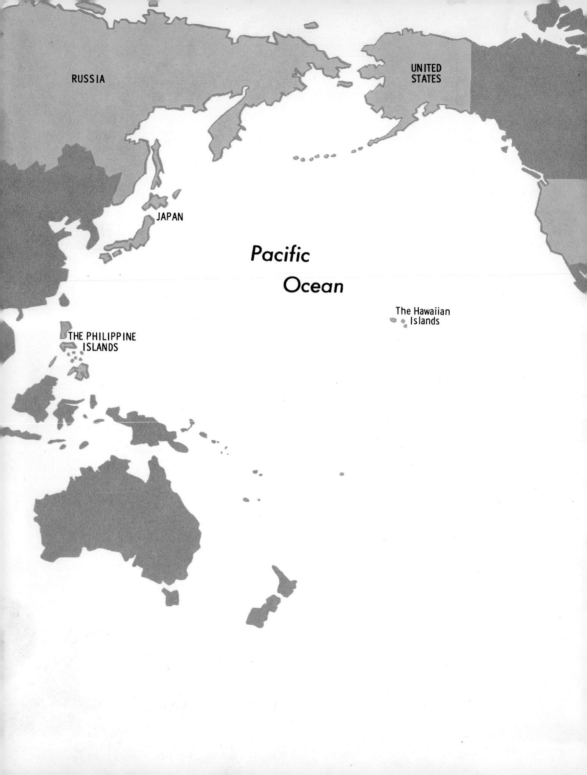

RUSSIA

UNITED
STATES

JAPAN

Pacific

Ocean

The Hawaiian
Islands

THE PHILIPPINE
ISLANDS